Alberto
GIACOMETTI

Notes

on

the copies

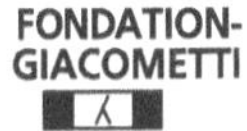

Notes sur les Copies

Après quatre ou cinq essais je m'aperçois qu'il
m'est impossible de donner une espèce de chronologie
de ces copies ce qui était le but de ces notes.
Toutes les copies se situent aujourd'hui comme
sur le même plan comme si l'espace avait pris
la place du temps, Elles font tellement partie
de ma vie, de mon activité depuis ma
plus lointaine enfance qu'en fait elles se
présentent dans ma mémoire comme elles
sont distribuées dans ce livre c'est à dire hors
de toute ordre Chronologique. Depuis toujours,
et de façon sûrement pour plusieurs motifs, j'ai
eu l'envie, le désir et le plaisir de copier soit
d'après des originaux mais surtout d'après
des reproductions Toute œuvre d'art qui me
touchait m'en thousiasmait m'entéressais
particulièrement, j'ai commencé à
copier avant même de me demander pourquoi
je le faisait probablement pour donner
une réalité à mes prédilections plutôt
à la peinture ici que celle ça mais depuis
des années je sais que le fait de copier

Notes on the copies

<u>4 October 1965</u>

As it is impossible for me to date precisely most of these copies, I shall try to give their basic chronology.

Since I have seen reproductions of works of art, and that goes back to my early childhood – it gets mixed up with my oldest memories – I felt the immediate desire to copy all those that attracted me the most, and that pleasure in copying has never left me since.

The copies reproduced are only a small part of all those I have made of which many are lost, especially those made from originals in small sketchbooks, and suddenly I see myself in Rome in the Borghese Gallery, copying a Rubens, one of the great discoveries of the day, but at that same moment I see myself simultaneously in my whole past; in Stampa next to the window around 1914, focused on the copy of a Japanese print, I could describe it in every detail, and in 1915, Rembrandt's *The Supper at Emmaus* and then a Pinturicchio that suddenly comes to mind and all the frescoes of the Quattrocento's paintings in the Sistine Chapel, but I also see myself [forty] years later coming back in the evening to my studio in Paris, leafing through books and copying this or that Egyptian sculpture or a Carolingian miniature, and also some Matisses.

How to say it all? All the art of the past, of all epochs, of all civilisations appears before my eyes, simultaneously, as if space has taken the place of time. Distraught, I stop, too many things to say and how to say them? The memories of the art works are mixed with personal memories, memories from my own work, from my whole life.

Somewhere I am still twelve, perhaps even I am especially twelve, but I don't know, I don't know! I wanted to talk about those copies, but I am incapable of doing so; I can look at them, I can remember them, but I don't know why, I cannot say anything about them or else I would have to relate my whole life, everything I remember.

And then what to say here, in the middle of this sea with no end, with no name, in the middle of this dark water in which I could sink, in which I could be eaten, devoured by blind and nameless fish.

I wrote this ten days ago on the boat travelling to New York, I reread it tonight on the journey back and I know now that it is mainly for these two crossings that I undertook this journey. I have barely looked at the sea since I saw, two days ago, the extreme tip of New York dissolve, disappear, fine, fragile and ephemeral on the horizon, and it is as if I was living the beginning and the end of the world, anxiety made my chest feel tight, I only perceive the sea surrounding me, but there is also the dome, the vast vault of a human head.

<u>18 October 1965</u>

For the fourth or fifth time, I try to give a chronology
to these copies but I don't know how to go about
it, and now I feel almost a repulsion, or at least a
resistance to talk about it.

No, I could easily talk about it, but not write about
it. I stumble on the difference between talking and
writing. 'From childhood… etc.' rather Stampa, bench,
table, book, image, copies, Borghese villa, studio, Paris,
evening, sofa, books, Egypt, Carolingian miniatures,
Louvres, Gudea 1923, elation. Simultaneously the arts
of all epochs, of all civilisations. I am on a boat, I'm
coming back from New York, tomorrow we will reach
Le Havre and Paris.

An impossibility to focus on anything at all, the sea
pervades everything, for me it is nameless although
today we call it the Atlantic. For millions of years
it didn't have a name, and one day it will no longer
have a name, endless, blind, wild like it is for me
today. How to talk here about copies of works of art,
ephemeral and fragile works of art that exist here and
there on the continents, works of art that come apart,
that wither away, that deteriorate day after day, and
of which many, and among them those I prefer, are
already buried, sunk deep into the sand, the earth and
stones, and all follow the same path. And all those
which before, have enthused me so much and that
I look at today almost with indifference, that fade

and clear out of my memory. Almost all precarious, defective, pretentious images and which after all I can do without; but at the same time all the moving and marvellous works that exist, innumerable, suddenly emerge. But often those particular ones have been the witnesses of the hardest civilisations, the darkest, the most oppressive and the one I loathe the most.

In reality, I no longer know what to think about anything and then each word I write is only the expression of my vanity, my pretension, my hypocrisy, yes, my gratification in shining, showing off, all 'attributes' I was already bursting with at the age of twelve. Fortunately, after there was a very long period of respite, in fact almost until these last few years, but now I am the one I was at twelve, no, not exactly, I made immense progress, now I only move forward by turning my back to the goal, I only do by undoing.

I don't know if I am an actor, a crook, an idiot or a very scrupulous boy. I know that I need to try to copy a nose from life.

After several attempts, I realise it is impossible for me
to give a kind of chronology of these copies, which
was the aim of these notes.

All those copies are today as on the same level, as if
space has taken the place of time. They are so part
of my life, of my practice since my early childhood
that in fact they appear in my memory like they
are scattered in this book, I mean outside all
chronological order. From the very beginning, and
that probably for several reasons, I felt the wish, the
desire and the pleasure to copy, from the originals
but most often from reproductions, any work of
art that moved me, enraptured me or particularly
interested me.

I began copying before I even wondered why
I was doing it, probably to give a reality to my
predilections, rather this painting than that one, but
for a few years now, I know that the fact of copying
is the best way to become aware of what I see, as it
happens in my personal work, I only know a little
of what I see of the external world, a head, a cup
or a landscape, by copying it. The two activities
complement one another, or did until recently,
for now I very rarely copy works of art. The gap
between any work of art and the immediate reality
of anything has become too wide and, in fact, only
reality interests me now, and I know that I could

spend the rest of my life copying a chair. Perhaps it was the purpose of all those copies and it is the very reason why I can no longer say anything.

'Notes sur les copies', in *Alberto Giacometti. Le copie del passato,*
Turin: Editions Botero, 1967 (text in French)
Pre-publishing of the text alone in *L'Éphémère*, no. 1, 1966

Is a copy anything but an attempt to extract the
maximum from an encounter with a work of art?
I'm convinced that the copy of a masterpiece is the
best school there is for any artist who decides to
make art. At all times, great artists have been aware
of that: Michelangelo made copies of Giotto and
Masaccio, Rubens of Titian, Ingres of Raphael, and
later, Delacroix of Rubens and Rembrandt, Manet
of Delacroix and Matisse of Chardin and so on.
In reality, there's nothing better than copying to
understand it has always been and will always be
about the same thing: art. And one discovers and
one learns art through art. Obviously I don't always
make copies of the whole piece; often, I capture the
part of the work that speaks to me the most. Look
at that landscape! Is it not the most magnificent
cubist landscape there is? Don't you think it contains
everything an abstract painting is likely to contain?
I made the copy of that landscape from a painting
by Jan Van Eyck – and it's only by copying it that
I realised how modern it is!

Extract from a conversation with Gotthard Jedlicka, 1953

At the Louvre with Giacometti
A conversation with Pierre Schneider

— What about going to the Louvre?

Giacometti accepts, out of politeness — he keeps his promises — rather than for pleasure. Does he abhor museums? On the contrary.

— I have almost the whole of the Louvre in my head, room after room, painting after painting.

In order to incorporate it, he has used the method employed by all Western painters since the Renaissance:

— I copied a lot.

— What?

— Almost everything that's been done since the beginning.

A place where one can see everything that's been done in art since the beginning constitutes, in short, a rather good definition of the ideal museum.
The Louvre is not as far from that definition as most museums. Giacometti visited it assiduously during his first years living in Paris ('every Sunday'). His preferences?

— What was the most immediate, the most recent: Chaldea, Fayum, the Byzantine period. I like from the past exactly what resembles most what I see, my vision of things. Like Chaldean sculptures. And I prefer Byzantine painting a thousand times to Western painting.

He was looking, drawing to sharpen his gaze:

— By trying to copy, one sees things better. I was
questioning intensely, each work at length, in turn.

*Seeing, questioning: Giacometti's approach is entirely
contained in those terms. He says:* 'To copy in order
to see better'. *So one senses he's ready to reduce art, his
art, to this activity: copying, representing as accurately
as possible something that is present. So simple it
becomes impossible.*

— Take the outline that goes from the ear to the chin:
how to represent on the canvas, on a distance of three
centimetres, a line that seems to be twenty centimetres
long? It's humanly impossible.

*Around 1923, sensing that absurdity led him to renounce
such a conception of art,* 'because it seemed to me absurd
to run after something that was doomed to fail totally
right from the start, you see?'
*Renouncing the questioning of reality, he attempted, for
a few years, to draw up an assessment of the certainties
it had deposited in his mind, abandoning to obscurity,
to quasi-abstraction the fragments he didn't succeed
in reconstituting — like an incomplete identikit. But
where does memory finish, and where does imagination
begin? His oeuvre gradually drew close to Surrealism, a
movement he seemed to have joined around 1930. For
it offered an alternative: to close those eyes that present
you with impossible tasks, to replace reality with the
imaginary, sight with vision.*

During that time, Giacometti stopped going to the Louvre; he only went back the day reality grabbed hold of him again. Was it all about to start once more, the same absurdity, the same impossibility? Yes, but for a slight difference which, to say the truth, is crucial: Giacometti discovered in the meantime that more terrifying still than the impossibility to represent reality is the unlimited possibility of non-representative art. Sight collides with the ridge of the external universe; vision projects without obstacle an internal universe on the screen of the canvas (or in malleable clay). Like a tyrant, it isolates, doesn't tolerate contradiction. Like a tyrant too, it suffers from that isolation, sensing that so much solitude will lead to its own downfall. Art, no longer having an object, becomes its own object. An odious thing for Giacometti for whom art is not the end of a vision but a means to see, a school for the gaze. (Indeed, I don't know any artist who perceives the elements of a work of art, painting or sculpture, with so much finesse and acuity, and one would deem that acuity to be contagious: during our visit, as soon as Giacometti stands before a painting, scrutinises it, immediately, people gather and imitate him.) One moves through a school by stages. The danger of art, as Plato noted, is that too attractive a teaching holds us indefinitely on the classroom benches. Giacometti doesn't think otherwise.

— In the past, I used to see through the screen of existing arts. I was going to the Louvre to see the paintings and sculptures of the past, and I used to find them more beautiful than reality. I used to admire paintings more than reality. Today, when I go to the Louvre, all those representations of the external world – because, up to fifty years ago, all painting and all sculpture were well and truly the direct representation of the outside world, right? – seem to me partial, precarious. I wonder how the hell they saw that. And what amazes me, what escapes me really, are no longer the paintings or the Chaldean sculptures but the woman I see leaning on a sculpture and looking at it. Immediately, the Chaldean sculpture becomes a pebble clumsily smoothed down that roughly represents a head. And the head that is staring at it becomes something dazzling that fills me with wonder, something completely foreign. I can only look at that person now, nothing else.

Reality only is capable of awakening the eye, of tearing it from its solitary dream, its vision, of compelling it to take on the conscious act of seeing, the gaze. For reality is the visible thing, and as jewels become dull when they are not worn, it seems it only lives in the converging lines of the gaze. An illusion? What is sure is that the mystery of its otherness pushes us irresistibly to question it. Here we are. Awkward questions, obscure answers, does it matter: what is being established, thanks to reality, is a dialogue.

— All of a person's activities are more or less unconscious, yes? Except for dialogue. Only dialogue with someone on something is of any interest, you agree?

It saves us from decisions, solitude, accumulation without a sense of resolution, sleep and forces those faculties of ours, quick to come to a halt, to be shared. According to

Giacometti, man is, for his own salvation, a being capable of dialogue. If he himself detests sleep, it is because in its recesses, one is always alone. He likes the places where one converses, and he willingly indulges in contradiction, including with himself, in order to revitalise the dialogue. He goes to the museum as one goes to the forum, the café; the works of art are partners in a dialogue. A continuous movement, almost tangible, is established between him and them. He moves forward, pulls back, re-enters the fray with so much enthusiasm that one could swear – and is it not like that, really? – they play opposite him. He converses with art like art (up to fifty years ago) converses with the visible.

That faith in the virtue of dialogue reminds us of the theory of modern economists for whom the health of an economy resides in the exchange, the continuous circulation of money. Should it stop, accumulate, lethargy descends and before long, it's the fatal crisis. So, as paradoxical as it seems, it's logical, even necessary to spend in a way that's unrecoverable. That active, fecund loss enriches. So one understands that Giacometti, while considering as doomed to fail the act of representing reality, deems it nevertheless useful, essential. Thanks to it, art is prevented from becoming an object and remains a medium of exchange.

I was expecting, after those words exchanged on the way, for Giacometti to drag me to the Sumerian sculptures or the Fayum paintings. He did nothing of the sort. After looking at the big Roman mosaic, the Amazonomachy, to signal the tragedy of man bleeding, he said:

— You know, what I most want to see is *The Cart* by Le Nain.

Disavowal of his old enthusiasms? No. Giacometti has questioned those works of art so much that they are simply part of him now. The dialogue is affected by it. One thinks of the two friends Nerval mentioned. They know one another so well that they guess the silent process of any of their thoughts; they have nothing left to say to each other and, if I remember well, content themselves with playing dominoes.

— Let's go up.

While we are climbing the stairs, I think about Giacometti's position in contemporary art: isolated because of that desire to represent, which connects him specifically to the art of the past. But that accuracy, which in other times could have been a facility, is now exactly its opposite. It's as if the heir to a long royal line felt compelled by an inner necessity to affirm his rights to the throne at the precise moment the people are knocking the crowns down or, an even worse fate, confined them to the pages of illustrated magazines. No help can come from those all-powerful ancestors. In the past, a tremendous naivety concealed the absurdity of the project that consisted in representing reality. Durer, Leonardo da Vinci, Seurat? A prodigious erudite naivety.
Our century got the better of this candid belief. Abstraction is perhaps just a simple wariness, the natural consequence drawn from our awareness that it's impossible to depict the world.
Giacometti shares this awareness. His venture is therefore even more preposterous. To persist in accomplishing, though he's disillusioned, an act whose courage to accomplish could only be given by a naïve faith.

— Are you really so isolated? Doesn't the subject of painting, above all the superficial agitation of subjects depicted, remain the same throughout the centuries? Last year in the gallery upstairs, there was a drawing by Poussin that Mondrian wouldn't have disowned. It's by turning a landscape upside down that Kandinsky discovered abstraction.

— That seems to me exaggerated. One says one works in the tradition and one makes the structure of the painting without the subject, as if the structure could be without the subject. As if there was a banal subject, incidental, superimposed on the painting.

— Rejoice, I can see the 'grand machines of academic art' upstairs, harbingers of a realism that must satisfy your wishes.

— Realism is so much rot.

— I beg your pardon?

— Those who come the closest to the vision one has of things are those that, in art, are called the great styles. Yes, the works of art from the past that I find most resemble reality are those that, in general, one deems the most remote from it—I mean the arts of style: Chaldea, Egypt, Byzantine art, Fayum, Chinese pieces, Christian miniatures from the High Middle Ages. And not at all what one calls realism, right? Or I should say, Egyptian painting is for me the most stylised. Any of us resembles much more an Egyptian sculpture than any other sculpture ever made. And it's the same thing for exotic arts, for African or Oceanic sculpture. People like them because they find them entirely invented and because they refute the outside world, the common view on reality. On the opposite, people look down on a classic head, a Greco-Roman, because it has a likeness, which is not very interesting at all.

I like sculpture from New Guinea because I find it resembles much more anyone, you or me, than a Greco-Roman head or a conventional head. Style gives us the most accurate vision. Of course nobody ever wanted to make style. For the Egyptians, that would have been completely meaningless. They were conveying as best they could the vision of reality. It was also a religious necessity for them; it was a matter of creating doubles as close to the living being as possible. A text exists, a poem of sorts that says there are sculptures so real they can frighten the people who see them. Style is another vision that reveals it. For us, Egypt is a style because we see differently. But for them, who only had their own art, who only knew – very badly, on top of that – certain arts from Asia, and who were not probably very interested in them either, there was only one clear vision of the world, theirs. And it was the same for the artists of prehistoric times, for those of the Roman times, for the Polynesians. They had no choice. Theirs was the one single acceptable vision of things. On the other hand, now, one knows all the visions possible and one calls 'styles' those visions halted in time and space.

*— The acuity, the accuracy of vision would then be the
condition of style?*

— Exactly. I know that if I could manage to make
a head just a little like I see it, that head would
inevitably become for the others what one calls style.
Of course, I haven't really succeeded yet. All the same,
there is in my sculptures something that is close to…
People who look at my sculpture think it is invented,
right? But what makes them look at it is the fact
that it truly comes closer, just a little, to my vision
of things.

— Realism…

— A realist painting is a painting not real enough
to become a style. Its flaw is that it doesn't resemble
anything.

*One understands now why the way Giacometti looks
at the museum is so much more inquisitive, penetrating
than ours. We are prone to consider that all is
accomplished once we have recognised the style in the
work of art; for Giacometti, on the contrary, the style is
only the sign of the existence of the work, but to perceive
its specific nature – and at the same time, what it is that
makes it appear to us an artistic style – one has to find in
it this part that is vision and representation of truth. But
Giacometti is going to give me a proof of that. We are
at the top of the stairs; on our right, Cimabue's* Virgin
Enthroned with Angels.

— This is the painting I liked the most, the one
I found the most real. Those brutes have put it on
the staircase, they have thrown it out of the Louvre.

We come closer.

— One doesn't make anything more real. Here… The
Roman excavations changed Giotto… Look here, one
doesn't make anything more real, more dense than the
hands, it's more real, truer than Rembrandt's hands.

*Something peculiar is happening: under that intense gaze,
the Virgin's hands are growing, it's the only thing I see
now, they isolate – I suddenly think about those sculptures
of my companion that only represent a foot, a leg, but so
huge, in appearance, that one no longer thinks about their
extension – they cut you from your surroundings.*

— What depth!

*We were looking for the aspect of one thing, we
unexpectedly encounter the depth of space. Dialectics
of opposites, of which Giacometti is, in his own work,
the (consenting) victim rather than the master; the
part becomes as big as the whole, the whole becomes
tinier than the small part, the will to represent precise
individuals gives birth to almost anonymous figures,
the need for discussion generates endless silent distances.
But those distances, Giacometti greets them with glee;
without them, painting is nothing but a decorative
diversion.*

— Today, abstract painters see everything in large format, strong colours, marks without depth.

Large format fails to concentrate the gaze, strong colours blind it, and the marks drown the precise identity, like a billowing of sumptuous materials hide the contours of the body. And without a neatly drawn, precise identity, there's no depth. It's the detail that differentiates, detaches, separates one form from others, isolates by creating what we call 'space'. In themselves, the infinities of space cannot be grasped, and to go further, as Pascal said, they are frightening. They need to be lured by a form, defined as fully as possible. Reciprocally, the artist will only access space unintentionally.
Like the fisherman looking for crabs, so busy beachcombing that he doesn't notice the sea rising around him until, finally looking up, he sees himself isolated on a rock, the artist searching for truth finds himself, without realising it, assaulted on all sides by depth. Marvellous but so dangerous that he has to hold on more firmly still to the appearance of things, which hollows the depth a little bit more…
So the discussion goes on and on in a perpetual movement.

— I see a tree more like Mantegna or Van Eyck than like the Impressionists, *he says in front of St Sebastian.* They work in depth, while the Impressionists see in marks. I was crazy about this painting. Because of the colours; there are few, very few, but it's the opposite of greyness.

With a touch of melancholy:

— This oeuvre is true, but it cannot be our path towards truth. Mantegna saw this head *(the archer's)* as I myself see heads. But I could never do it like that. It's like the *St Sebastian* is behind a curtain. We won't be able to lift it ever again. *(Silence.)* What is extraordinary is that each discovery is always immediately lost forever.

Would style just be the vision after the curtain has come down? In any case, no contradiction between them. In front of Da Vinci's Bacchus:

— First, it looks real, then it looks like a sign; both dancing Buddha and swastika.

But this lesson is far too didactic. The most intimate part of Giacometti's approach is revealed in the following remark:

— And then, as a contradiction, those flowers, at the bottom. *(One needs to lean forward to make them out, they are so fine, so fragile even.)* This is more real and stranger than Dürer, a little piece of China in Milan. *(A pause.)* Those stems: tall like trees.

The East has supremely possessed the art, so close to Giacometti's dialectics, of making the immense come out of the delicate, and the infinite through the means of a strict finitude.
The dancer from Bali moves with his knees bent, almost crouching; when he stands up straight, it looks like he's performing a prodigious jump. The effect of jumping forth

*is greater than with a dancer from the Russian ballet
who never stops jumping. In front of Goya's* Marquesa
de la Solana*:*

— How wonderful! It's done with the least possible
means, it's as little coloured as Mantegna, but how
dazzling it is!
Next to them, David and Ingres seem awful.

*Isn't Giacometti keeping up a continuous exchange with
culture because it teaches us, by sharpening our way of
looking through multiple confrontations, to distinguish
between differences more and more minimal, to reduce the
scale of visual stimuli without weakening the intensity of
their effects on us?
In a densely populated neighbourhood, the square's meagre
vegetation sings as clearly as the luxuriant flora of jungles.
By overcrowding our consciousness, culture—and that's
another lesson from China—makes us more attentive to
the slightest variations. It's useful to us on the condition
we don't try to use it. When we do so, we get entangled
in the curtain. The cultural distance curiously resembles
that which Giacometti wants to find in art. And when he
marvels in front of Corot's* Woman with a pearl, *we no
longer know, in the end, if it's to one or the other or to both
that his brief comment refers, proffered in a nostalgic tone:*
A strange eye… far away… far away…
*Similar to the characters in his oeuvre, Giacometti, who
goes to the Louvre because he needs a dialogue, finds
solitude there. But that which precisely makes contact
impossible, creates the field of art: the space in between,
the depth. A painting from the past is as remote, no more*

no less, than the tree or the model we want to represent.
In front of Tintoretto's Self-portrait*:*

— One doesn't get closer, it always remains at a
distance, like reality. It's one of the paintings in the
Louvre I liked the most when I arrived in Paris. He is
the only one to come close to the Fayum, to Byzantine
art. He goes further than Rembrandt (as for Cezanne,
he goes elsewhere). It's the whole skull: the eye, but
also the eye socket, the structure of the head itself.
And it's made with nothing. It's the most beautiful
head in the Louvre, really.

Finally here's the object of our stroll: Louis le Nain's
The Cart.

— After what we've just seen, it's a little dull, limited,
a minor subject.

But Giacometti's gaze persists, and already judgement is
replaced with dialogue, perspectives change, are reversed.

— It grows on you immediately, no? One thinks of
Chardin, Vermeer… It's sharp like the lash of a whip…
What a wonderful figure! *(the one in the background,*
on the left)… The one on the right looks more fake…
No, not more fake: it's seen in a different way. *(Under*
the gaze in search of truth, of the identity of things, they
separate.) The pigs, the group on the left, the landscape
and the group on the right are painted in three
different ways. It could be three different painters.
The woman with the bucket is so beautiful that it's

already a whole painting, one cannot even look at the character next to her. *(A pause, a silence, which is like the answer, in the one who's looking, of the depth that is hollowed between the various parts of the painting, isolated in their truth – of that depth which, through another reversal, will connect the disparities, like the sea unites the islands between which it circulates.) Then:* It's composed nevertheless.

While Giacometti is talking to me I see, becoming clearer, implicit behind Le Nain, his own work, as if the disinterested candour of his gaze was making the curtain transparent. What he teaches me about his art he could never have told me without the mediation of that other. For it only concerns Le Nain, whose Peasant Family in an Interior *is there in front of us. Immediately the true to life quality of the details that capture the attention and in its expanding beam:*

— The little red in the wine glass gives colour to the whole painting. Without it, it wouldn't exist. The candlestick on the table: it's tall like a monument on a square in Rome.

Indeed, it's no longer a corner of the tablecloth but the Piazza Navona that I see. But already he adds:

— What friendly faces! … And the eye of the girl is really Fourth Dynasty… And the head of the old woman resembles the heads of mad women in Géricault, the heads of Rembrandt, Corot, Chardin…

*— Talking like that at a time when the attention to detail,
the anecdote is considered incompatible with art!*

— I couldn't care less!

*As dissimilar as they might be, the relationship with
reality and the relationship with art have, in the painting,
an equal presence and are reconciled.*

— The eye is black and at the same time, it looks like
Piazza Navona, like the Fourth Dynasty. Everything
is equally real. The wine pot placed on the table and
the glass that the man holds vertically above the
other, that's been done already; however, he repeats
the scheme of the superposition of the characters
in *The Cart*.

*Consubstantiality of the artistic style and the vision of
reality which, at the edge of the living gaze, doesn't lead
the present vision to hide away in the art world, but to
bring the works of art from the past to the present of the
vision that is incarnated in this precise moment in some
paintings.*

— It resembles everything… and nothing.

*Nothing because gradually the depth is imposed in which
are reabsorbed the neat forms that generated it.*

— A pleasing depth, which one enters like music.
It's so pleasant, so delightful.

*Musical, nocturnal depth of the space in which, losing
their identity, those faces so interesting earlier, are now
no longer anything but anonymous spheres, discreetly
radiant. The images of reality are lamps that shed light
for a moment on the dark room of the space. Fatal power,
for the reawakened space soon devours them, crushes
them with the whole weight of their isolation. In front
of* The Peasant's Meal*:*

— That man on the right, exhausted, adrift, as if lost in
the desert.

*But that loss is worth more than all the successes. We glance
at the next painting, one by Antoine Le Nain:*

— Good painting, beautiful surfaces, but not those
planets in space, that music.

*And while the inflexible row of museum attendants
advances towards us, pushing us to the exit, we look at*
The Cart *for the last time.*

— It is though, because of its colour, one of the
paintings I like the most. It's finished perfectly.
Because of the cut wood on the left – it's like a little
island floating away. From afar, for me it's in one
colour… The colour of the countryside. Oh yes! Yes!

'At the Louvre with Alberto Giacometti',
Preuves, no. 139, September 1962, p. 23-30

<u>For 15 days now…</u>

For 15 days now I've been trying to paint landscapes.
I spend all my days in front of the same garden, the
same trees and the same background. I saw that
landscape for the first time one morning, radiant in
the sun, the trees covered in blossoms, and in the
background, far away, the mountains covered in snow.
That's what I wanted to paint but since then the sky
has been less limpid, it's often raining, I haven't seen
the mountains in 15 days, the blossoms are gone, the
whites and the lilac, and I carry on with my landscapes
till night.

Each day I perceive a bit more that I see hardly
anything and I no longer know how, by which means
I could put on the canvas something of what I see.
Any hope of representing the vision of the first day
has gone, but I'm quite indifferent about that. The
landscape should only be a beginning, it's the one
I have all the time in front of my eyes, outside my
studio door, I've seen a lot of others in the area
that I've also wanted to paint, I started one, one day.
I thought I could make a whole series of landscapes in
the morning, in the evening, some with big ensembles,
others with a few trees, others still with the river.

But I no longer think about it, those in front of my
door would be sufficient for months and I should
probably be forced to reduce it further still, first to
a part of that landscape, then probably to one single
tree, to end with one single branch. That I should do
the landscape or some flowers in a vase, or the vase

with the dry flowers, or the vase alone, or a few other objects that are there on the table, is no longer of any importance. Or a figure in the room with the objects that surround it, and I would go back quite quickly to the same subject I've been trying to paint for years and the landscapes would once again be postponed, or in any case I don't see when I could go further than the one I see from my window or outside my door.

But I see all those I would have liked to paint, around my studio in Paris, then Malakoff's wasteland and the surroundings of Paris, Dieppe and the Cap Ferrat, but also all the land towards Digne. And here, just beyond the Italian border.
In the evening, I often look at all the reproductions of landscapes I can find in the books I have here (it's a rather limited choice) in order to know which attract or interest me most. I compare them and copy them. There are a few reproductions by the Impressionists, the Dutch and Flemish primitives, the Egyptians, an album of Chinese landscapes, and that's more or less all.

What remain in my memory tonight are above all the Cezannes, the Chinese paintings, the Ruysdaels and the Van Eycks as well as the Egyptians, that which will probably remain in the memory of almost everyone, at least of almost every painter.

Finally I reduce my choice to two details in Van Eyck, an Egyptian relief, two or three Chinese landscapes and the Ruysdaels. They are the ones that seem to

me the most lifelike, especially the Van Eycks and
the Egyptian relief, and also a cascade among the
Chinese rocks. It's almost embarrassing talking about
Chinese landscapes today, for they are so much talked
about, admired for the atmosphere, the space, the
vagueness, though they seem to me rather sharp and
precise like a stone.
In the end, these are the only three (works) that attract
and interest me. I copy them and it seems to me they
have something, even a lot in common.

The painted landscapes which come first to my mind.
The vast and horizontal landscape in the Crucifixion
by A[ntonello] da Mes[sina], the three high crosses
behind that peaceful and wonderful landscape; the
black crows in the sky in V[an] Gogh.
The Ruysdaels.
The trees on the small enamel plates in the Art Mosan
section at the Louvre.
The trees on the Giotto in the Louvre.
The landscape by V[an] Eyck in the Louvre, which
attracts me, which amazes and annoys me a little.
The big Chinese leaves at the Guimet Museum.

That's almost all that comes back to me of all the
landscapes I have seen, and three reproductions here,
two backgrounds in V[an] E[yck], a Chinese painting
and an Egyptian relief, and that's all.
No, a vertical Tintoretto, M[aria] M[agdelena]
under a big tree at the Sch[ool] of S[an] R[occo],

and Seurat, a little bit of everything and his drawings,
the modern ones.
The Braques, Matisses, Derains and Bonnards and
Jongkinds, and the Corots, and the Renoirs and
Cezannes [at] least, and the Altdorfers and D[erains]
and F. Grubers and Soutines, and that's all.
And V[an] d[er] Wydens and Brueghels, and that's
all and a very old V[an] G[ogh], a shack at night with
a light, and that's all.
That's all
and the little Brouwers
and that's all.
Yes, that's all.
Nothing more comes back tonight, but it seems to
me that there are others that escape my attention but
which ones, the Rembrandts, the little ~~Berlin?~~ with
the ice skating ring, and many Dutch? and V.M.?
no Italians except the ones mentioned?
Oh yes, the antiquities at the Louvre, and others
I know through reproduction, the two little Romans,
on top of everything I mentioned.

But tomorrow evening I shall copy the three that
I have badly reproduced here, and nothing else?
The Utrillos and Ro. are also coming now
This boat won't go far if they insist

To sing them han han
Han and hin
like some ki ka ki,…

Landscape! landscape, morning sky, evening sky,
always golden there,

essentially how to say, one cannot say, one needs
to paint the
big liquid skies and to have them and the t r e e s!
the trees, the trees

The whole matter is solved in painting, in sculpture
and in drawing.
The landscape that echoes in the background
inside me, oh, of Ant[onello]
da M[essina] at the bottom behind the three high
crosses in the peaceful sky and the green of the
meadows, crying over it like Mary between…

Around 1952

'One can suppose that realism consists in copying… a glass as it is on the table. In reality, one never copies anything but the vision that remains of it at each moment, the image that becomes consciousness… You never copy the glass on the table; you copy the residue of a vision.'

Extract from a conversation with André Parinaud, 1962

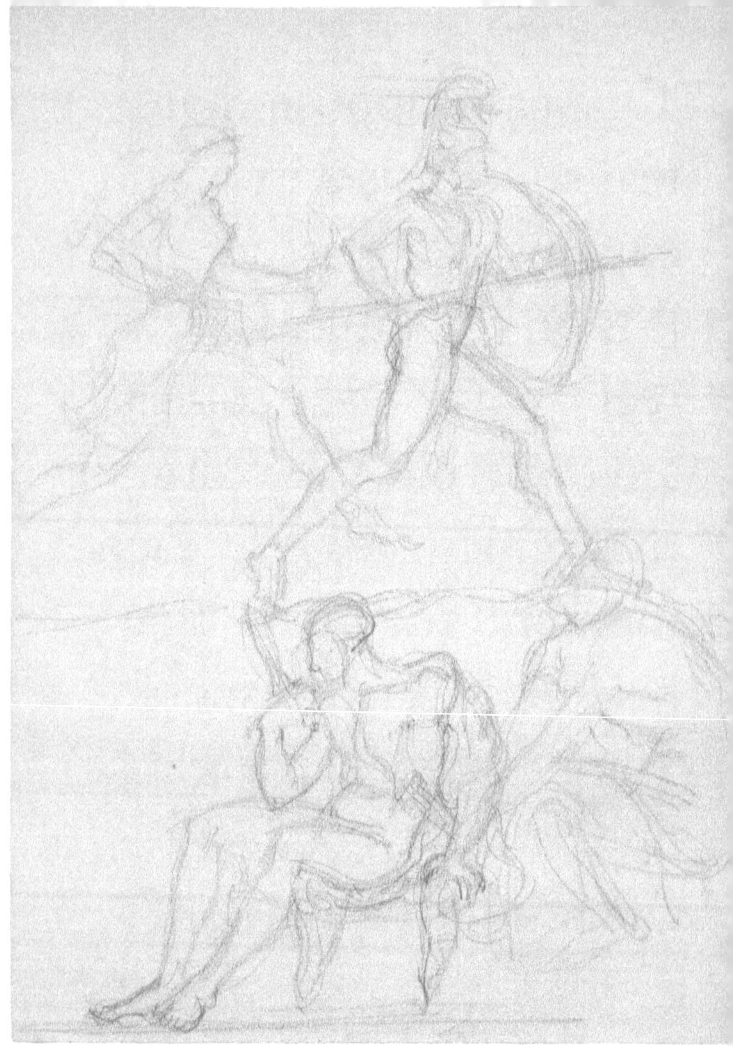

Copies from a Greek vase, 1942
Lead pencil on vellum paper, 34 x 25 cm
Fondation Giacometti

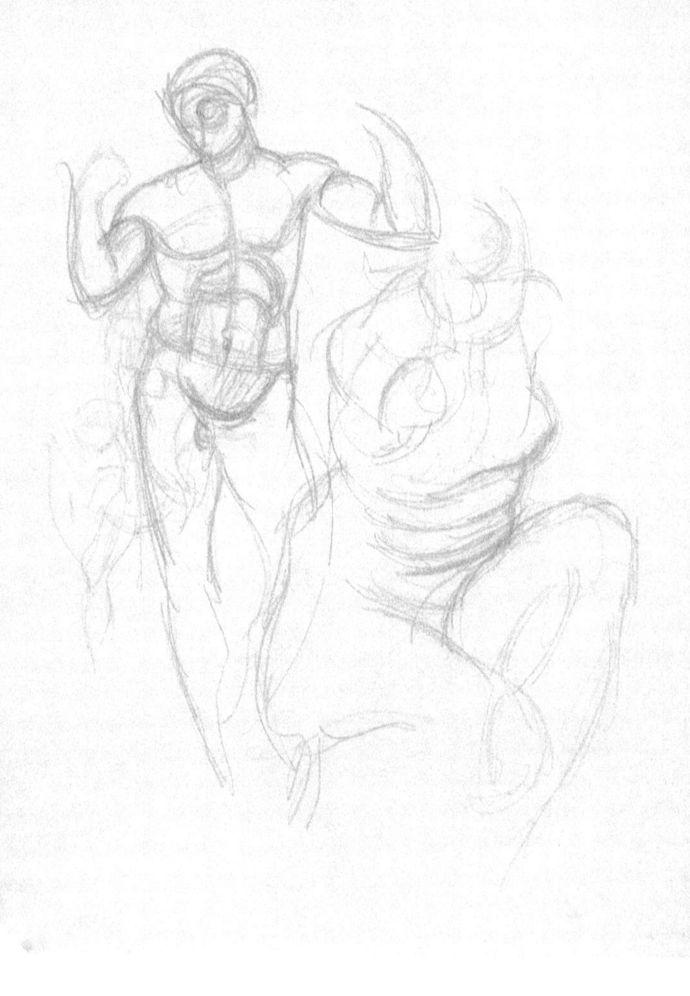

Copies from Polykleitos's *Diadumenos*
and Doidalsas's *Crouching Venus*, 1942-1945
Lead pencil on writing paper, 27 x 21 cm
Fondation Giacometti

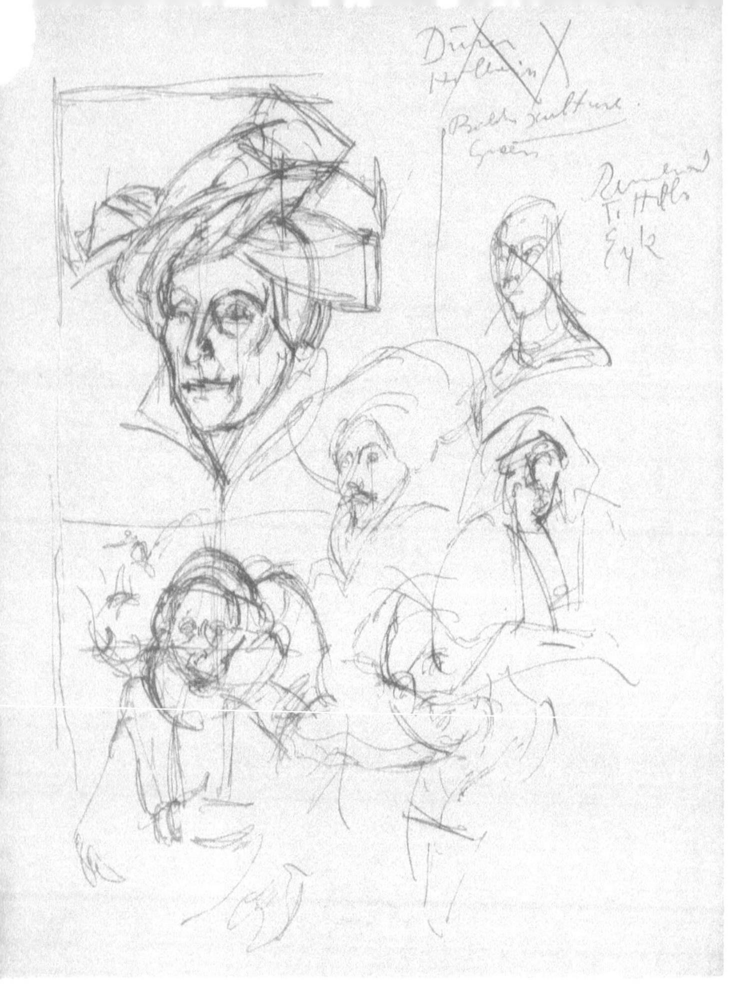

Copies from Jan van Eyck's *Portrait of a man in a turban*
and Pierre Paul Rubens's *Self-portrait*, 1942-1945
Black ink on writing paper, 27 x 21 cm
Fondation Giacometti

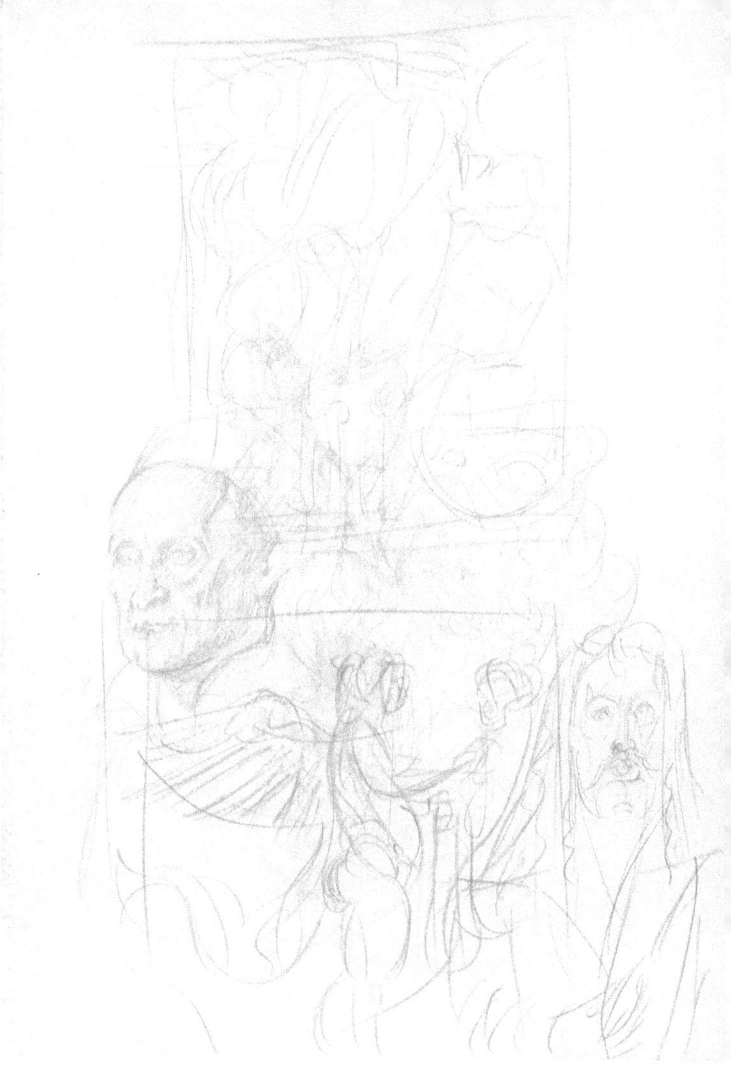

Copies from *Portrait of Jakob Muffel, Nemesis,*
Self-portrait and *Melancholia* by Albrecht Dürer, 1942
Lead pencil on loose page from notebook, 41.5 x 29.5 cm
Fondation Giacometti

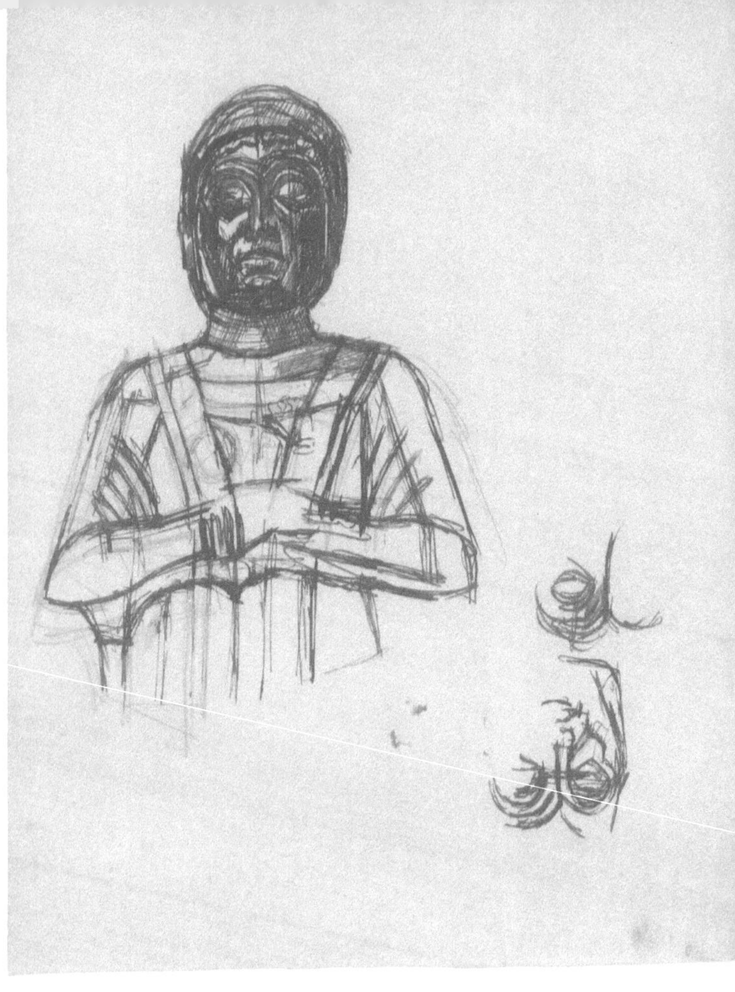

Copy from a Sumerian statue:
Woman with scarf, 1935-1937
Blue ink, lead pencil on writing paper, 27 x 20.9 cm
Fondation Giacometti

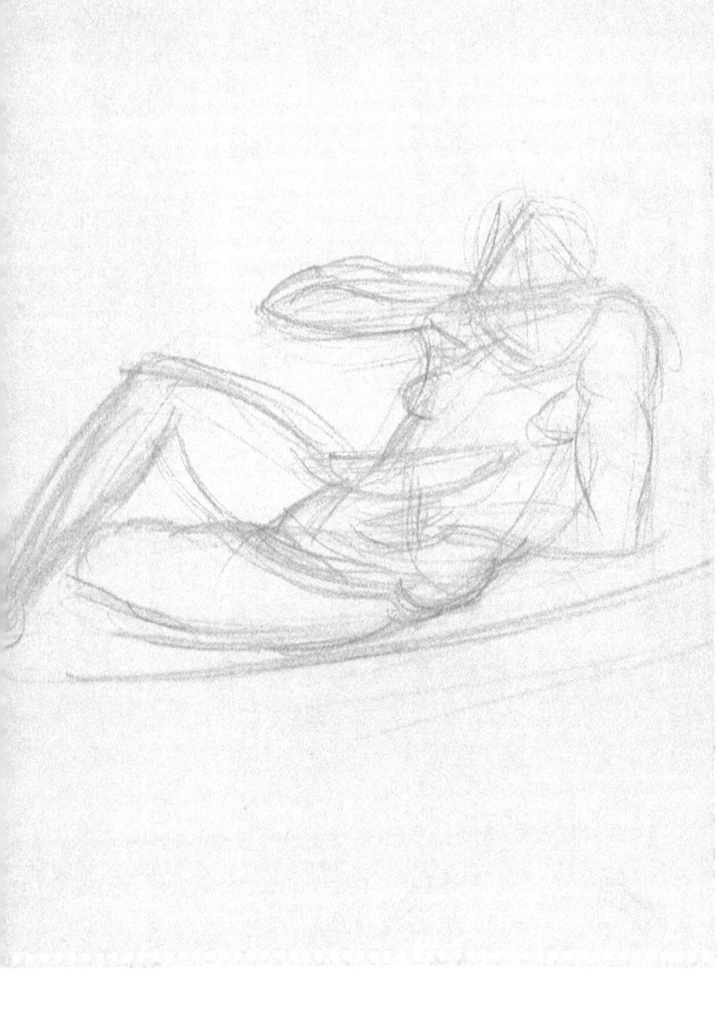

Copy from a chalice krater with red-figures
painted by Euphronios: *Drinking hetaera*, 1942
Lead pencil on loose page from notebook, 29.5 x 30.8 cm
Fondation Giacometti

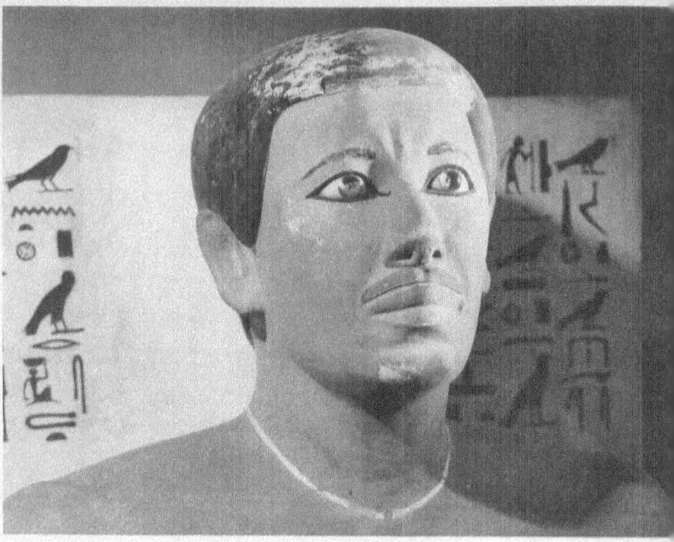

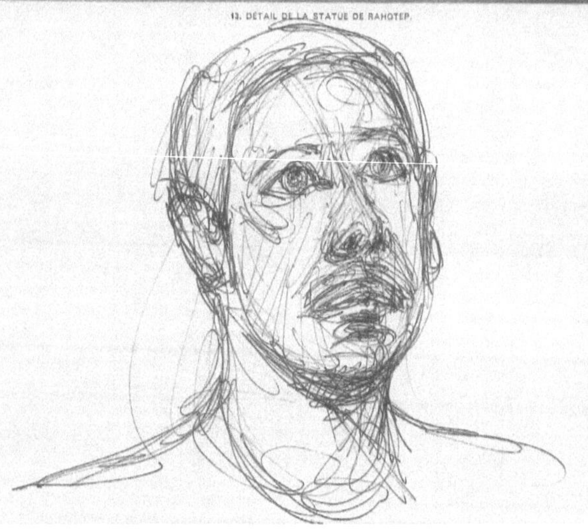

13. DÉTAIL DE LA STATUE DE RAHOTEP.

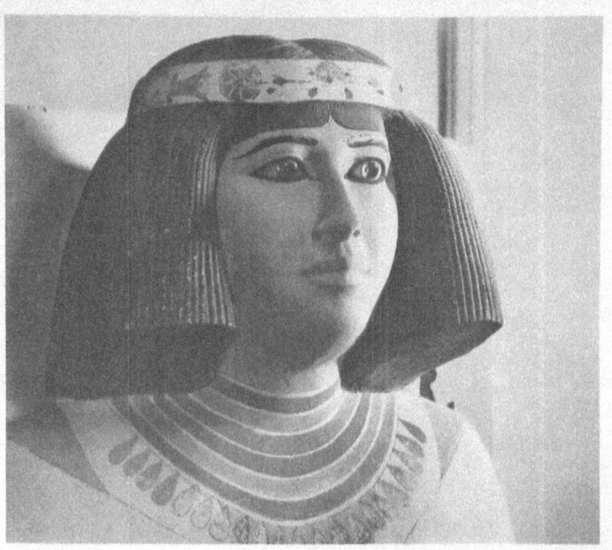

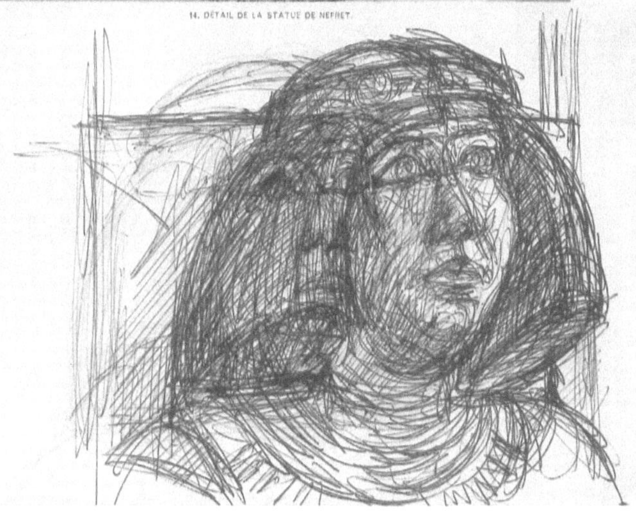

From Egyptian sculptures: *Head of Rahotep*
and *Head of Nofret*, in *Encyclopédie photographique
de l'Art.* Le Musée du Caire, from 1949.
Blue ballpoint pen on pages of magazine
Fondation Giacometti

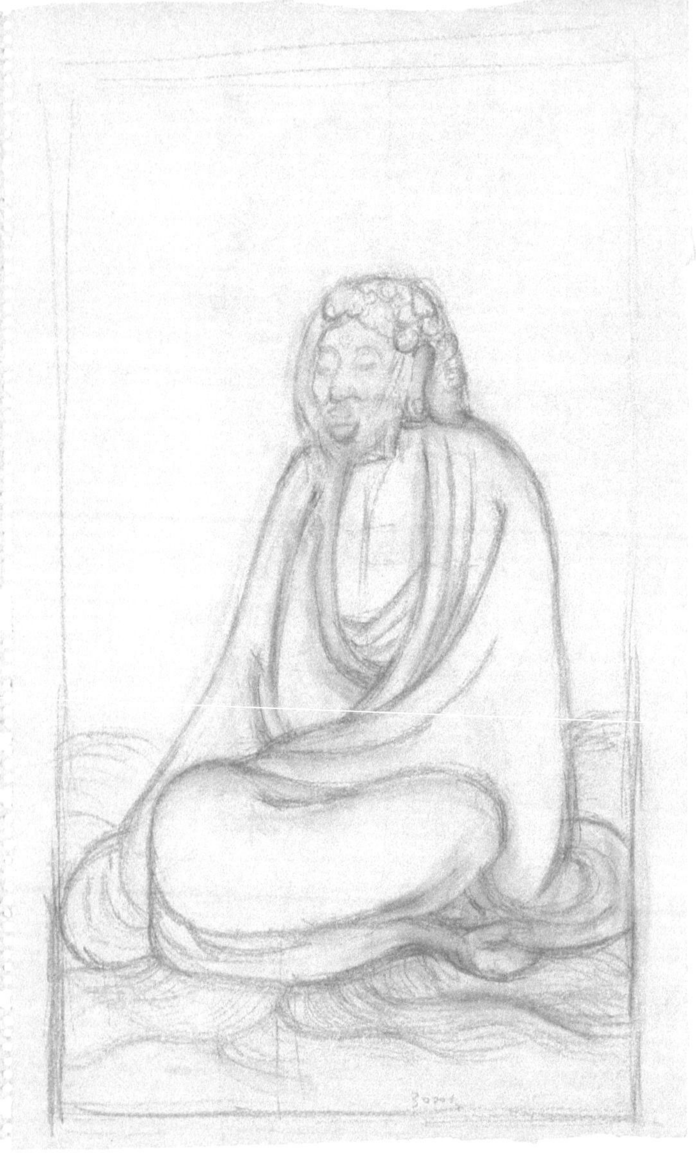

Copy from *Sakyamuni sitting in Zen meditation* by Li-Long-Mien, 1942
Lead pencil on loose page of notebook, 34.2 x 21.7 cm
Fondation Giacometti

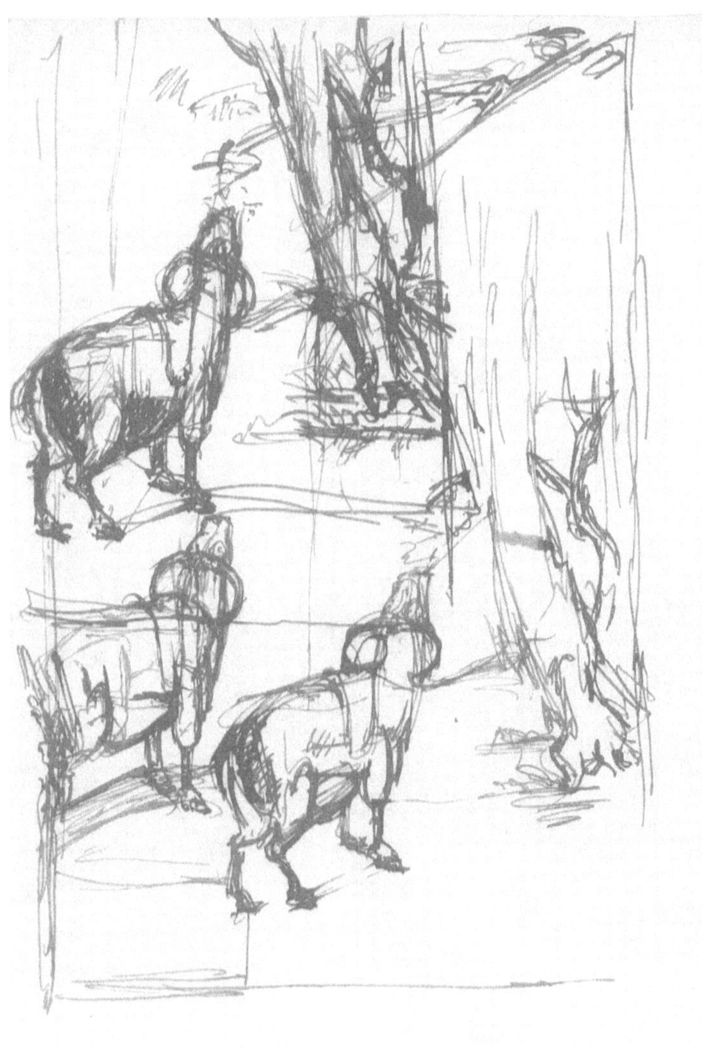

Copy from *Water buffalo grazing on a leaf*
by Chang Fang-Ju, 1942-1945
Blue ink on writing paper, 21 x 14.8 cm
Fondation Giacometti

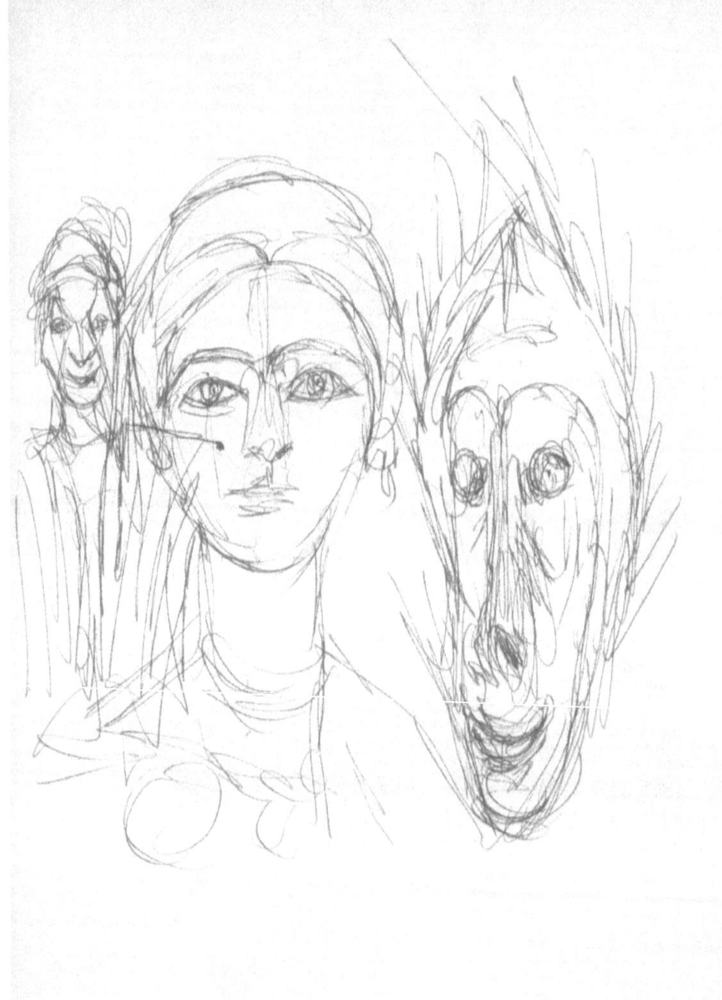

Copies from a rambaramp funerary effigy from Malekula,
portrait of a Fayum mummy and a Sepik mask from
Papua New Guinea, 1956-1957
Blue ink on writing paper, 29.5 x 21 cm
Fondation Giacometti

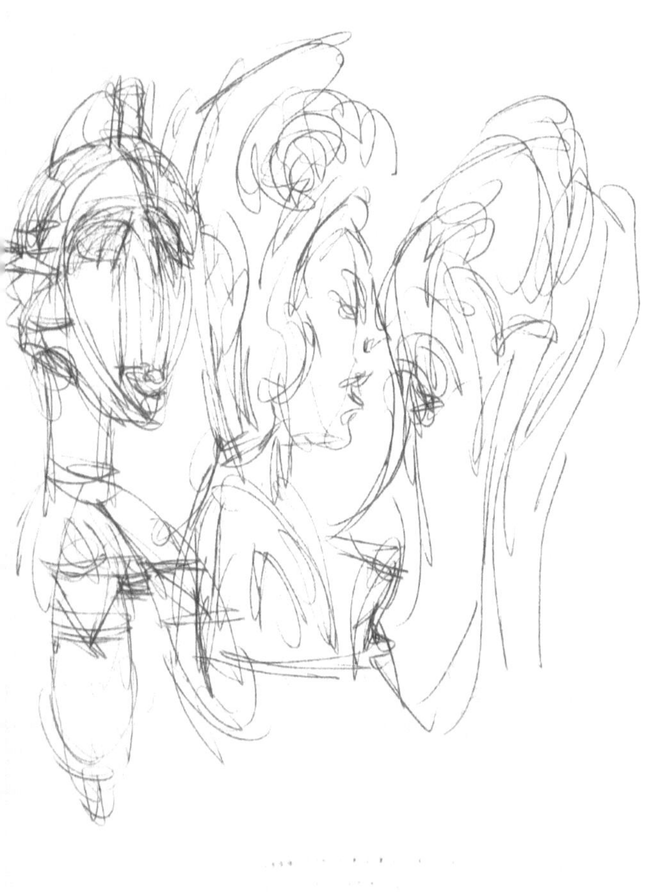

Copies from a Nimba Baga shoulder mask from Guinea,
a statue of the Maya maize god from Copan and a Guro
mask from Ivory coast, 1956-1957
Blue ink on writing paper, 29.5 x 21 cm
Fondation Giacometti

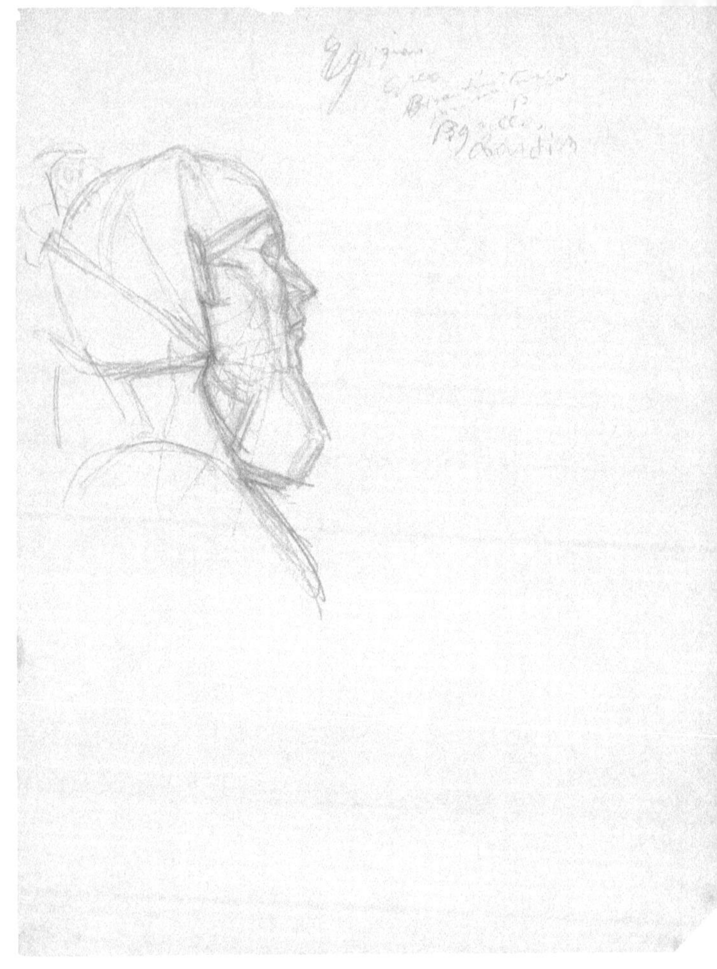

Copy from the statue of Khafre, 1942-1945
Lead pencil on writing paper, 27 x 21 cm
Fondation Giacometti

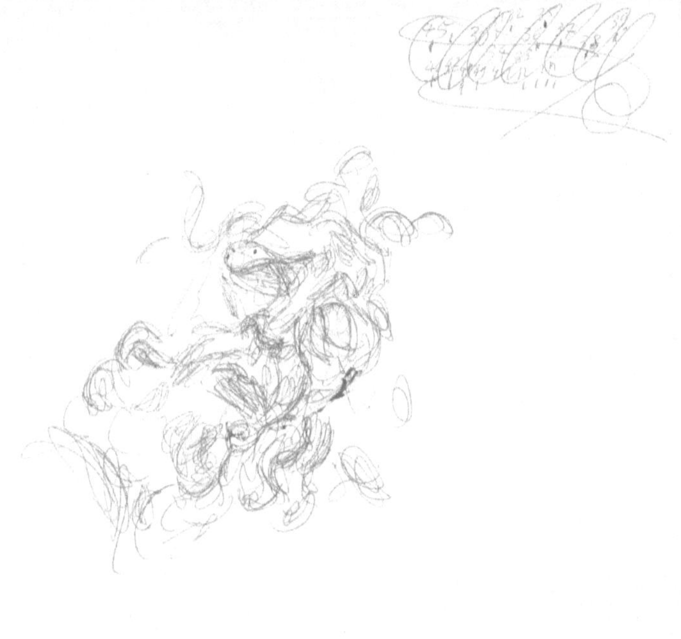

Copy from a detail of *Laoccoön and his sons*, c. 1959
Blue ballpoint pen on writing paper, 29.5 x 21 cm
Fondation Giacometti

<u>Is Greek art modern?</u>
<u>A conversation with</u>
<u>Georges Charbonnier</u>

— Mr Alberto Giacometti, the figures that you draw or that you model in paintings, in sculptures, provoke in some an amazement that doesn't always seem to us to be justified. We saw, in the exhibition that was held a few years ago at the Louvre, the figures of the Etruscans, figures that strangely resembled yours. And I remember, in Athens, in the museum, having seen some of those silhouettes that were flat and seem to me to establish, if you want us to start with this, a certain relationship with your preoccupations. Does what I've just said seem to you exact as far as your art is concerned?

— It's difficult to answer that, I don't know the Greek sculpture you're talking about, I'd really like to discover it…

— It's an Athena.

— Which must come close, in sculpture, to some other flat sculptures I know very well. On the other hand, as far as the Etruscans are concerned, I think it is a likeness that is due to chance, and not something that goes further, because the three or four Etruscan sculptures that were exhibited at the Louvre, those heads were modelled round like classic sculptures, and the bodies elongated, but I wonder if those elongated bodies were not made for ornamental reasons, if they were not really objects.

— They were objects.

— Objects, because next to them were small sculptures, entirely in the proportions of archaic Greeks; with exactly the same heads as the elongated figures.

— As for you, do you consider that it is a necessity on your part, a way of seeing, which is in a way, imposed on you?

— Not even! It is not exactly that, I never willingly wished to make elongated or slender sculptures. I always wanted to make them–I still want, actually–I want to make them as close as possible to what I see, how I see them. By wanting to make them this way, in spite of myself, entirely in spite of myself, they became elongated, as before they became tiny. They only became real, until a certain period, when they were tiny, they were only becoming for me a little real when they were elongated, and I fought that elongation for years.

— Yes, and to what extent perhaps the Greek art we are talking about can be of any help to you, or can be a model, an inspiration?

— In Greek art, as in all the arts of the past, what strikes me, what pulls me up each time is, of course, what seems to me the most real in relation to my vision of the outside world.

— And in what works of art do you find them then?

— To keep to the Greeks, there are works that go from the very first archaic pieces to the very last like

the *Laocoön*, or the Farnese *Gladiator*, which dates
back to the first century BC. So through the whole
of Greek art there are things that move me or make
me passionate in equal measure. What moves me in a
Cycladic head are the flat Cycladic heads…

— Which we think about obviously.

— Where there's barely the indication of details.
At first sight, there's just a nose, but it seems to me
one of the most lifelike heads, the most lifelike in
reality compared to my vision of a head. So it moves
me, and the fact that it is for example, flattened,
makes me see, or makes me understand a little better
my vision of reality.

*— We understand it very well at the same time as you, but
then, the* Laocoön *that you mentioned earlier?*

— And the *Laocoön*, which obviously has entirely
different qualities than the Cycladic head, moves me
as much, at this moment I could even say it gives
me more.

— Why?

— It's quite hard to say. The Cycladic head gives the
impression it is the closest to the immediate vision,
the instinctive vision, from the outside.

— One certainly has to believe that since art began like that.

— Yes, it's felt like that, it is not thought or reconstructed, it's made the closest to vision, it's the reason why, for example, it is inevitably flattened, because at a certain [distance], one cannot at the same time seize the tip of the nose and the neck in its depth. You see the width of the face, and you lose the depth, or the opposite, and that doesn't happen just in archaic Greek sculptures, it happens in almost all the arts, the Negro sculptures.

— It's a flat face.

— On the other hand the *Laocoön*, the torso.

— Yes, we are in the third dimension here.

— It's the torso in particular that moves me.
The whole piece, but it's especially in the torso
that it's happening.
To be able to seize a volume, such a dimension in
a movement in space requires a huge knowledge,
a knowledge that amazes me much more than
the vision of the archaic.

— It's perhaps the reason why so many people have walked away from it.

— Yes, they've walked away from it because it has become completely foreign to us.

— Yes, that's why I was so happy to hear you say…

— A hundred years ago they were masterpieces,
the masterpieces of global art. The *Laocoön* which
was placed at the top of the stairs facing *Victory of
Samothrace* was very visible, now it has been dethroned,
it's in the room downstairs.

— *It's doing penance.*

— Where one can barely see it. It's a sign of the times.

— *Disaffection.*

— Yes, but it is not because we no longer look at it
today or we consider it has stopped being interesting,
that it has really stopped being that!

— *Obviously.*

— The extraordinary qualities that are in those
sculptures, in the precise way we are rather more
attracted to archaic or primitive things, interest me.
I won't say I like them more, they interest me or they
move me more because of those qualities.
For example, there's the structure that comes
from the depth, in *Laocoön*'s torso.

— *Yes.*

— It all comes from the inside, it's like balls of nerves.

— *It's made from the inside.*

— All is in movement, it all gives the impression of [movement].

— *A movement which, nevertheless, seems to us at times, if not rigid, at least fixed.*

— No, I'm not talking about the imitation of movement, I'm talking about…

— *Yes, of course, the internal movement.*

— The movement of the mobile thing itself.

— *Which creates the stillness.*

— It's like thrusts of forms, from the inside to the outside.

— *And force.*

— Which become force, which become violence, in a way. I revisited, looked at all the Greek sculpture, or almost. And it would have sufficed for me to see today and for a long time, simply the eye, an eye of Homer's bust, which probably is a sculpture entirely from the last period, if it's not even an antique copy. What we find, and it impresses me today, the construction of Homer's eye is already the construction of all Byzantine painting.

*— Through an incursion in time, we have understood,
I believe, better than in any other way the relation that
exists, and that you feel so strongly, between an art that is
represented in the Louvre and your art.*

'Analyse spectrale de l'Occident'–l'art grec est-il actuel?
Recorded on 27 March 1958 and broadcast on 16 April 1958

'My paintings are copies of reality that haven't succeeded.'

Extract from a conversation with Antonio del Guercio, 1962

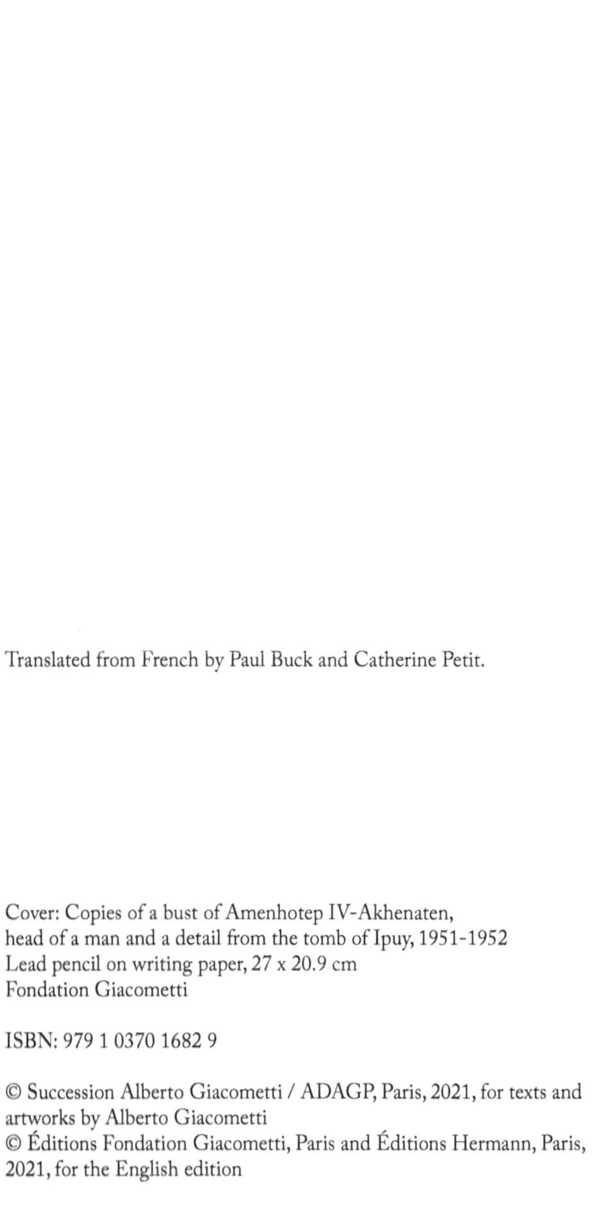

Translated from French by Paul Buck and Catherine Petit.

Cover: Copies of a bust of Amenhotep IV-Akhenaten,
head of a man and a detail from the tomb of Ipuy, 1951-1952
Lead pencil on writing paper, 27 x 20.9 cm
Fondation Giacometti

ISBN: 979 1 0370 1682 9